👤 _____

✉ _____

📱 _____

GREATER THAN A TOURIST BOOK SERIES REVIEWS FROM READERS

I think the series is wonderful and beneficial for tourists to get information before visiting the city.

-Seckin Zumbul, Izmir Turkey

I am a world traveler who has read many trip guides but this one really made a difference for me. I would call it a heartfelt creation of a local guide expert instead of just a guide.

-Susy, Isla Holbox, Mexico

New to the area like me, this is a must have!

-Joe, Bloomington, USA

Good information to have to plan my trip to this destination.

-Pennie Farrell, Mexico

Great ideas for a port day.

-Mary Martin USA

Aptly titled, you won't just be a tourist after reading this book. You'll be greater than a tourist!

-Alan Warner, Grand Rapids, USA

Even though I only have three days to spend in San Miguel in an upcoming visit, I will use the author's suggestions to guide some of my time there. An easy read - with chapters named to guide me in directions I want to go.

-Robert Catapano, USA

Great insights from a local perspective! Useful information and a very good value!

-Sarah, USA

GREATER THAN A TOURIST –BALI INDONESIA

50 Travel Tips from a Local

Hanum Gitarina

Cover designed by: Ivana Stamenkovic
Cover Image: https://pixabay.com/en/indonesia-bali-ulun-danu-1578647/

Greater Than a Tourist
Visit our website at www.GreaterThanaTourist.com

Lock Haven, PA
ISBN: 9781983271267

>TOURIST

50 TRAVEL TIPS FROM A LOCAL

BOOK DESCRIPTION

Are you excited about planning your next trip?

Do you want to try something new?

Would you like some guidance from a local?

If you answered yes to any of these questions, then this Greater Than a Tourist book is for you.

Greater Than a Tourist- Greater Than a Tourist- Bali Indonesia by Hunum Gitarina offers the inside scoop on Bali. Most travel books tell you how to travel like a tourist. Although there is nothing wrong with that, as part of the Greater Than a Tourist series, this book will give you travel tips from someone who has lived at your next travel destination.

In these pages, you will discover advice that will help you throughout your stay. This book will not tell you exact addresses or store hours but instead will give you excitement and knowledge from a local that you may not find in other smaller print travel books.

Travel like a local. Slow down, stay in one place, and get to know the people and the culture. By the time you finish this book, you will be eager and prepared to travel to your next destination.

TABLE OF CONTENTS

10. Diving sites
11. Rafting
12. Temples
13. Sangeh, the monkey kingdom
14. Kintamani
15. Batu Bulan village
16. Tenganan village in Karangasem
17. Jatiluwih Bali
18. Tampak Siring Palace
19. Safari park, botanical garden and Marine Park
20. Bali Bird (and Reptile) Park
21. Garuda Wisnu Kencana
22. Menjangan Island
23. Nyepi Festival
24. Ngaben Festival
25. Trunyan Village
26. Gitgit waterfall and other hidden waterfalls
27. Legian the place where pop-culture resides
28. Saraswati garden

Local Cuisine and Best Restaurants

29. Balinese crispy ducks and other ducks menu
30. Betutu
31. Babi guling (Suckling Pig)
32. Jimbaran seafood restaurants
33. Balinese yellow rice
34. Sate or satai

NOTES

DEDICATION

This book is dedicated to everyone who loves to experience the world and all of its beauties. Especially for my life companion, Faith, and Mikayla, let's travel, visit new places, meet new people, understand new cultures, taste new food, and bring back many valuable memories. We are the citizens of the world, do not only live in one place.

ABOUT THE AUTHOR

Traveling is my passion. I love exploring the beauty of my country, Indonesia, especially Bali. I have been to Bali for so many times, learning that every trip was unique and unforgettable. There were always new things although you visited one place for so many times. Therefore, I really want to share some great spots of Bali that you really have to visit with the hope that you will return back home and tell everybody on how wonderful this place is.

HOW TO USE THIS BOOK

The Greater Than a Tourist book series was written by someone who has lived in an area for over three months. The goal of this book is to help travelers either dream or experience different locations by providing opinions from a local. The author has made suggestions based on their own experiences. Please do your own research before traveling to the area in case the suggested places are unavailable.

FROM THE PUBLISHER

Traveling can be one of the most important parts of a person's life. The anticipation and memories that you have are some of the best. As a publisher of the Greater Than a Tourist book series, as well as the popular 50 Things to Know book series, we strive to help you learn about new places, spark your imagination, and inspire you. Wherever you are and whatever you do I wish you safe, fun, and inspiring travel.

Lisa Rusczyk Ed. D.
CZYK Publishing

OUR STORY

Traveling is a passion of the "Greater than a Tourist" series creator. Lisa studied abroad in college, and for their honeymoon Lisa and her husband toured Europe. During her travels to Malta, an older man tried to give her some advice based on his own experience living on the island since he was a young boy. She was not sure if she should talk to the stranger but was interested in his advice. When traveling to some places she was wary to talk to locals because she was afraid that they weren't being genuine. Through her travels, Lisa learned how much locals had to share with tourists. Lisa created the "Greater Than a Tourist" book series to help connect people with locals. A topic that locals are very passionate about sharing.

9

WELCOME TO
> TOURIST

INTRODUCTION

"Travel is fatal to prejudice, bigotry, and narrow-mindedness, and many of our people need it sorely on these accounts. Broad, wholesome, charitable views of men and things cannot be acquired by vegetating in one little corner of the earth all one's lifetime."
— *Mark Twain*

As one of the most popular tourist destinations in the world, Bali should be on your traveling destination list. This place is located in Indonesia and known as the island of paradise. Others also call this place as the islands of god and goddess for it has many temples and religious ceremonies, beauty sceneries, rich cultural heritages, fertile lands, and friendly people.

When traveling to Bali, you need to invest many; not in capital, but in time and energy. Although the island is quite small, there are so many spots to visit, culinary to taste, and cultural heritages to witness. One or two week trip in Bali won't be enough for there are so many surprises that the island offers.

The tips presented in this book mainly come from those who have experienced Bali and know the detail

13

of every corner in the place. You won't waste your time and even your money because this book gives you more than any guides found on the internet. Enjoy!

Accommodations and Transportations

1. VIBRANT LIVES

For you with young spirits and adore dynamic lives, you should choose to stay in Kuta. Kuta is a region in Bali where pop culture exists. Pubs, nightclubs, cafes, five stars hotels, contemporary galleries, and other hangout places scatter everywhere. However, there are also small alleys in Kuta region where you can find cheaper accommodation. The thing is, when you want to experience Bali for 24 hours a day and 7 days a week, Kuta is the best place to stay. Kuta also has a famous beach called Kuta beach that is famous for its beautiful sunset.

2. QUIET ATMOSPHERE

Sanur is just the opposite of Kuta. Many tourists choose to stay in this area because it has relatively more peaceful atmosphere. This place is so perfect for anyone who wants to visit Bali with family members, especially those with kids. There are also various types of accommodations that you can choose, from luxurious hotels to bed and breakfast. The lowest room rate in Bali cost you for approximately $20-$30 per night. Some places apply "bule price" which means slightly higher rates for foreigners. One more thing, Sanur has many small beaches for you to enjoy sunrise.

3. HILLY AND GREEN VILLAGE

For you who wish to experience a real getaway, you may choose to stay in this village, Ubud. Surrounded by rice fields and green hills, this high land of Bali is a perfect place to escape from your busy life. Although there aren't many options of accommodation in this area (compare to those of Kuta and Sanur), you can literally find great accommodations that blend seamlessly with the nature. Do not imagine high storey buildings with many rooms in a single alley, Ubud has many cottages and resorts—and some offer private swimming pool and outdoor Jacuzzi—that truly make you feel at home.

4. CAR AND MOTORCYCLE RENTALS

Real travelers don't take taxies (although it is OK to take them occasionally). It is advisable to rent a car, motorcycle, or scooter. All you need to have is an international driving license. However, if you don't have one, you can go to a Police Station in Denpasar to get a temporally driving/motorcycle permit which valid until three months. If you don't speak Bahasa Indonesia, you'd better ask a local to provide you with an interpreter service (contact your hotel, they will absolutely help you with this). Good tips for you: always negotiate the price when you rent any vehicle in Bali, and ask whether the price include any insurance. One more thing, you can also hire a private tour driver along with the car in a package for approximately $100-$150 (depending on the type of the car) for 10 hours (with $10-15 of extra per hour cost). The car can occupy 4-7 people. For motorcycle or scooter rent, the price is about $8-$20 (depending on the type and the duration of renting).

5. HOTEL TOUR SERVICE

If you are a first timer, you can use this service that is usually provided by most hotels in Bali. You can start with a one-day package to make yourself familiar with Bali roads and traffics. The tour is usually grouped based on the activities you wish to perform, for example adventurous tour, water sport tour, cultural tour, and many more. However, you can also request a special tour (for example a combination of several packages at once) with different prices of course. A one-day tour usually cost for about $40-$100 (depending on the hotel) per person, including lunch and drink, entrance fee for all destination spots, insurance, a tour guide, and of course tax.

"People who don't travel cannot have a global view, all they see is what's in front of them. Those people cannot accept new things because all they know is where they live."

—Martin Yan

Tourist Attractions—from Breathtaking Scenery, Exquisite Cultural Experiences, Adventurous Activities, to Sacred Traditional Festivals

6. FAMOUS BEACHES

There are two types of beaches in Bali—famous and unspoiled beaches. The famous beaches include Sanur (famous for its beautiful sunrise), Kuta (seeing a romantic sunset and many hangout places afterwards), Lovina (watching dolphins), Nusa Dua (high-end private beach), Dreamland (relatively unspoiled and clean but quite far from the main city of Bali), Geger beach (clean and safe), and many more. The beaches are usually categorized based on the activities you can perform, for example surfing, culinary, party, sunbath, romantic dinner, etc.)

7. HIDDEN AND UNSPOILED BEACHES

Some hidden and unspoiled beaches in Bali have great tourism potentials. However, you have got to prepare yourself with enough food, drinks, and other supplies for there are only few stores or sellers there. Some of great hidden beaches in Bali include: Perasi /Virgin beach (famous for its white sand), Balangan beach (surfing spot), Green bowl (difficult to reach, quiet, the heaven for pro surfers), Amed beach (diving and snorkeling), Dream beach (a small island in the eastern of Bali), Karma beach (a bit expensive and very exclusive), Finn's beach (beautiful scenery, cable lift, great food), Balian beach (black sand, surfing), and many more. To reach those places, you need extra efforts for most hotel tour services do not include them in their package. Asking a tour guide to take you there is better, otherwise, you can always ask local people for direction.

8. SURFING POINTS

Every beach has unique waves' characteristics. Therefore, surfers categorize the surfing points based on the character of the waves and the level of surfing expertise. There are beaches for beginners (including Kuta, Legian, Seminyak, Batu Golong-Canggu), intermediate/experience (including Kuta reef, Nyanyi/Muara, Madewi, Tukad Balian, Biaung,

Segara, Sindhu, Matahari Terbit, Berawa, Echo, and many more), or professional surfers (including Uluwatu, Suluban, Impossible, Keramas, Bingin, Dreamland, Padang-Padang, and Parerenan). There are also surfing schools for beginners to practice riding the waves. If you are lucky, you can watch international surfing championship (check out Bali surfing calendar).

9. WATER SPORTS

If you wish to challenge yourself with some water sports other than surfing, you can visit Tanjung Benoa. Teens and young people usually love this place (well, I can say that most kids also love this place but they will feel disappointed for some water sports require certain age or height to be met). You can enjoy snorkeling, sea walking, banana boat, parasailing, wakeboard, water-ski, jet-ski, scuba diving, donut boat, flying fish, and many other breath taking activities here.

10. DIVING SITES

Talking about water sports and activities in Bali is endless. When it comes to diving, Bali has great diving and scuba diving spots as well. Some of them are Liberty Ship Wreck, Manta Point (observing Manta Ray closely), Crystal Bay (spotting the

magnificent and rare Mola Mola), and Secret Bay
Gilimanuk (great spot for underwater photographer).

11. RAFTING

Bali also has several famous rivers that become
tourists' favorite spots to do rafting. The first one is
Telaga Waja River which offers you quite
challenging rafting and tracking adventures. The
second one is Ayung River where you can go slowly
along the river to enjoy great green scenery.

12. TEMPLES

There are many temples in Bali, such as Tanah Lot,
Besakih, Uluwatu, Ulun Danu Beratan, Pura Luhur
Lempuyang, Pura Taman Ayun, and many more.
Every temple has different and unique characteristic,
so I suggest you to visit at least some of them to see
the difference. For me myself, I have two favorites.
First is Tanah Lot in Tabanan Bali, mainly because it
is located on the coast, to be precise is on the top of a
tall crag so that it provides the sense of serenity—and
really beautiful indeed. Tanah Lot is also famous for
its mass traditional dance and musical drama called
Kecak, performed by at least 150 performers. And the
second is Ulun Danu Beratan because it is located in
the Beratan lake with beautiful mountainous scenery,
so you can rent a boat and enjoy a perfect evening
there.

13. SANGEH, THE MONKEY KINGDOM

It is a famous forest in Bali where many monkeys live and protected. Local people think that the monkeys are sacred animals. Therefore, they are treated like kings. Visitors are allowed to give some foods and snacks to the monkey. You can really touch them in their habitat, but you don't need to worry because they are friendly. It is also located near to Denpasar (only 30 minutes drive). The weather is also cool and nice there.

14. KINTAMANI

This is the name of a village where Batur Mountain Caldera is located. This is also the place where Batur lake and Ulun Danu temple are located. Visitors are not likely to stay in this place. They usually go around the place and explore all the tourist destinations in that area in a one day visit by car or motorcycle. There is also a local vehicle called bemo (an open van) which can take you around for less than $2.

15. BATU BULAN VILLAGE

If you wish to experience some of the greatest traditional dances in the world, you should come to this village. People in this village have two dances to perform: Barong and Keris. They are performed daily in several local stages in the village. However, for you who don't like to witness sharp traditional weapons being stabbed in someone's body, don't sit in the front row. Another famous village is Peliatan which is famous for its Legong Keraton dance and fabulous gamelan instrument.

16. TENGANAN VILLAGE IN KARANGASEM

Anthropologists said that this village is one of the most secluded societies in Indonesia. Although many domestic and international tourists come and go, the people are still wearing traditional clothes, perform traditional way of lives, speak only local languages, hold traditional ceremonies regularly, and preserve traditional houses. It is the picture of the native of Balinese society—a must visited place while in Bali.

17. JATILUWIH BALI

From ancient times, Balinese people has one of the most sophisticated technology of field's irrigation system called terasiring or paddy terraces. The farmers have an irrigation association called subak, which has called international attention for its ability to renew the condition of polluted lands and increase the farming productivity. In Bali, the paddy fields are arranged in such ways so that all farmers will not experience any water shortage. You can experience walking along the terraces, chasing ducks, enjoy beautiful atmosphere and fresh air. Besides Ubud, you can also visit Jatiluwih village to experience the great man-work of paddy terrace. There are also some restaurants where you can rest for lunch in an outdoor setting. So relaxing, refreshing, and increasing your appetite.

18. TAMPAK SIRING PALACE

Bali has long been acknowledged as a national treasure. This palace was built in the era of Indonesia's first president as the place for the president and his family, as well as his international guests to rest while enjoying the beauty of Bali. Don't forget to take a chance to cleanse your body with the holy water provided in this place. It is so refreshing. But don't forget to bring extra clothes because you may get your body wet.

19. SAFARI PARK, BOTANICAL GARDEN AND MARINE PARK

Do you want to play with the elephants, ride on their backs, feed, and bath them? You must visit Bedugul safari park and botanical garden or bali safari and marine park. Those places are very suitable for family recreation spots because you can introduce your children with the nature while learning about animals.

20. BALI BIRD (AND REPTILE) PARK

Here, you will meet thousands of birds from hundreds of species. You can take pictures with five or six kakatoa exotic birds at once—feel the sensation of having some birds standing on your head, shoulders, and palms. It is a perfect place to take your kids for a walk while learning about the beauty of tropical birds. You can also see some rare birds including kasuaris, indonesian owls, and the famous Balinese jalak birds. You can also encounter with some of the biggest and oldest reptiles in the world, the Komodo Dragons. Have some fun too by letting a big snake slither all around your body—but you can always miss the chance and try other fun thing to do in this park.

21. GARUDA WISNU KENCANA

Garuda Wisnu Kencana is a cultural park where you can see sculptures made by Balinese artists. Many said that it is a perfect photography spot for you can capture a moment when traditional cultures meet modern technique. Many couples choose this place as their pre-wedding photography venue because of its picturesque scenery. For me, it is the place where my camera finds its best friends.

22. MENJANGAN ISLAND

Menjangan means deers. This island is the habitat of Balinese deer. You can see them wandering around the island, interacting with locals and tourists. It is also the best diving and snorkeling spot with relatively shallow water and colorful corals. I personally haven't visited this place for it is located in the far north west of Bali Main Island and should be reached by boat (approximately 7 hours from Denpasar). Locals say that this place is a must visited place while in Bali, especially those who want to experience a totally different underwater world. it is a truly perfect place to escape from the busy world.

23. NYEPI FESTIVAL

Nyepi is when Balinese Hindus celebrate their new year. When you visit Bali in this day, you will experience a total shock. Unlike other New Year celebrations, Balinese Hindus do not do any activity in this day. They cannot lit fire, cook, go out from the house, turn on electronic devices or even lamps at home, or even open the window. It is a complete silence. Offices and shops are usually closed for 24 hours. There are only some "guards" that will go outside and act as "the eyes" for everyone else. The Balinese Hindus believe that the day was a day to purify the macro and microcosm (the universe and the self). For some people, they will do tapa brata or meditation. However, two or three days before Nyepi, there is a mass ritual in which people march with big statues of the gods and evils and offerings were brought to the nearby lake or beach to be thrown away. If you really wish to witness this cultural event, you must search over Google by typing Nyepi and the year of your visit (e.g. Nyepi 2016).

24. NGABEN FESTIVAL

Another culturally rich festival is Ngaben or the burning of the dead. It is usually performed in mass rituals when the families of the dead people dig up the graves of their ancestors, bath them, and place them in a high bamboo tower (at least 9 meters or more). The bodies were then burned and the ashes were scattered in the sea. There are many rituals performed in this event. The preparation usually involves so many people and needs at least one month. Ngaben is maybe one of the most expensive rituals performed in Bali. Therefore, some people perform Ngaben together to cut the budget. Tourists usually love to see the march of the towers with the coffins inside as well as the burning rituals.

25. TRUNYAN VILLAGE

Not all Balinese will be burned after they died. In a village called Trunyan, dead bodies are not buried nor burned. They were placed on the ground, under a big

Trunyan tree. Amazingly, they don't smell at all. Although I personally refuse to visit this eerie village (I mean, what is so interesting about seeing dead bodies lied on the ground?), but many said that the village is beautiful and the people are friendly. This place has attracted many researchers, anthropologists, and sociologists to investigate about the unique culture.

26. GITGIT WATERFALL AND OTHER HIDDEN WATERFALLS

Feel the sensation of fresh water and cool scenery. Gitgit waterfall is located near to Lovina "dolphin" beach. Usually, tourists only visit Gitgit for it is the most popular waterfall in Bali. However, you can try some of these waterfalls that are more beautiful and breathtaking. My favorite is Tegenungan waterfall. The waterfall is not so high but the scenery is so amazing. A communal shower consists of several pipes is also available there if you wish to experience an open air shower like what the ancient Balinese do. Other waterfalls are Gunung Kuning, Nungnung, Munduk and Melanting, as well as Carat. It is advisable to come in the morning and play in the water while the sun is not so hot. It is not advisable to come in the evening for most of the places are so remote.

27. LEGIAN THE PLACE WHERE POP-CULTURE RESIDES

If you want to experience Bali nightlife, Legian is the best place to visit. There are many pubs, clubs, bars, and cafes. You can also find restaurants that serve many kinds of food from all over the world. There are also many art shops where you can purchase traditional souvenirs. Legian also has a famous beach called Seminyak. Not only that, you can also see the Bali Bombing museum.

28. SARASWATI GARDEN

It is also one of my favorite destinations. This garden is actually a temple to worship the goddess of art. So, you can imagine how beautiful the temple is. I advise you to enjoy this magnificent temple in the morning or evening. You will spend a perfect morning walk in this spacious temple.

"I am often tired of myself and have a notion that by travel I can add to my personality and so change myself a little. I do not bring back from a journey quite the same self that I took."

—Somerset Maugham

Local Cuisine and Best Restaurants

29. BALINESE CRISPY DUCKS AND OTHER DUCKS MENU

Ducks are so popular in Balinese cuisine. You can have it fried or roasted with some secret traditional ingredients that make the taste of the ducks different from any of western ducks. The best place to eat duck is in Bebek Tepi Sawah restaurant and Bebek Bengil restaurant (I've been there and the place is so cozy with reasonable price).

30. BETUTU

It can be made of either ducks or chickens. They are wrapped inside banana leaves with some local herbs, roots, and seasonings, and stuffed with some cassava leaves. The taste is just exotic. However, if you are not familiar with spicy and hot stuff, you'd better order the salty version of this menu.

31. BABI GULING (SUCKLING PIG)

I don't eat this one, but my friends all said that you must try this signature dish of Bali. Many restaurants and food stalls offer this menu as their specialty. It is babi guling Bu Oka that becomes the best place to eat the dish. There are many Bu Oka franchises all around Bali, but you can be sure that they all taste great.

32. JIMBARAN SEAFOOD RESTAURANTS

Jimbaran is a perfect dinner place in Bali. You can enjoy a perfect evening with the whole members of your family, eat delicious seafood, and enjoy beautiful sunset in the beach. Choose the restaurant that gives you the best outdoor experience. You can eat with your feet touching the sand and the great magenta sky as the background. My tips: search over the internet to find the place that you desire, and don't forget to check the price. Ask some locals if necessary, or contact your hotel receptionist to give you some hints.

33. BALINESE YELLOW RICE

Yellow rice is cooked by using turmeric, coconut milk, salt, chicken broth, and other ingredients. It is usually served with scrambled eggs, fried mashed potatoes, fried or roasted chicken or duck, crispy and spicy stirred soya bean cake or anchovy, cucumber and tomatoes. All is served in a single plate, typically for lunch. It is one of my daughter's favorite (many Indonesian kids love the rich tastes of this dish)

34. SATE OR SATAI

It is like kebab which is roasted or grilled in the skewer. Satai is so popular in Indonesian cuisine. Almost all regions in Indonesia have their own version of satai. However, the version of satai in Bali is slightly different. Balinese uses minced fish or chicken to be attached around the skewer and with grated coconut as the wrapper. A mouth watering dish I may say, especially when served with peanut sauce and Indonesian soya bean sauce.

35. BREM BALI

Brem Bali is a traditional Balinese alcoholic beverage. The taste is sweet and light. Usually, Balinese people drink this beverage in a gathering or hangout event. You don't drink Brem Bali on the dinner table. This drink is sold in various different prices. My suggestion is always buy the bottled version sold in the registered store. Don't consume the beverage traditionally made by locals that is stored in drums and plastic container for the level of the alcohol may be too high.

"The traveler sees what he sees, the tourist sees what he has come to see."

—Gilbert K. Chesterton

Some Useful Tips

36. ALWAYS BARGAIN

Whether you are in a traditional market, art shops, or vehicle rentals, always bargain to get the best price. If you are not a good price negotiator, ask them to give you "the fix price." So, whenever they open the transaction with a certain price, just say "What is the fix price?" In Bali, the bargain usually starts with approximately 30% lower than the offered price. However, there are also places where price negotiation is impossible (usually when they have already attached a barcode on the product).

37. ALWAYS BRING EXTRA CLOTHES EVERYWHERE

You may not know what short of adventure you will experience while visiting some great spots in Bali. Although there are many clothes shops around the famous tourism destinations, you can't always buy new ones when you get wet or dirty. You will also have to prepare extra sandals or shoes (the most comfortable ones in your collection) for traveling around Bali requires a lot of walking.

38. PREPARE AN INTERNATIONAL DRIVING PERMIT

Before you go, prepare your international license so that you can rent a car or scooter. Although you can have a tourist driving permit that valid for 3 months in the local Police station with relatively cheap price (only about $20), the process to obtain one is so complex (mainly because of the language barriers). You will need to spend for about 2-3 hours only to get it.

39. MAKE A DAILY PLAN

Although Bali is a small island, there are so many spots to visit and adventures to experience. My suggestion is to make a daily plan, especially when you have only a short visit in Bali. For the best experiences, don't visit too many places in a day (just like what most hotel tours offer). Before your arrival, choose several best destinations that you wish to visit. Consult them with the locals (find one who work in the hotel) so that you can map your journey (be an efficient traveler). If you are an adventurer, dare yourself to explore Bali deeper and further.

40. BUY A LOCAL CELLULAR PHONE NUMBER AND ALWAYS HAVE YOUR HOTEL CONTACT

It is best to buy a local cell-phone number and keep your hotel phone number for a safer journey. You can also ask for local police hotlines (usually 110 or 112) but for quicker response, ask your hotel management about the number of the nearest police station.

41. DON'T LEAVE VALUABLE BELONGINGS IN THE HOTEL

Valuable belongings like passport, jewelry, wallet and money, or even cell-phone and camera should not be left in the hotel, especially when you stay in small inns or motels. Not only will it trigger crime, but it is also for your own interest and safety. Small accommodations aren't usually equipped with safety standards like 24 hour security guards and CCTVs. Prevention is the key.

42. BEWARE OF TRADITIONAL RITUALS AND CEREMONIES

Bali is the island of god and goddess. The people hold traditional rituals and customs strictly (not only because they want to attract tourist). So, you must also put a great respect on the traditions. Balinese people put offerings in every corner of the street, in front of their house, inside the hotels, on the beach and other places every day. Don't ever dare to step on it or play with the offerings. Locals will not respect that. It was also evidence of mystical power disturbing the people who show disrespect of the local traditions and rituals.

43. OCCASIONAL TRAFFIC JAM

Traditional ceremonies in Bali often involve hundreds or even thousands of people. This will create traffic jam. Therefore, when you are trapped in this occasional traffic jam, just enjoy yourself. Pull over and you can witness great cultural ceremonies performed by local people.

"The traveler was active; he went strenuously in search of people, of adventure, of experience. The tourist is passive; he expects interesting things to happen to him. He goes 'sight-seeing.'"

—Daniel J. Boorstin

Where to Shop, What to Buy

44. CELUK VILLAGE

Celuk village is the heaven for the female shoppers, especially for jewelry lovers. In this place, you can find handcrafted silver and gold jewelries. Tourists will find many jewelry shops and workshops where they not only can buy but also see the process of making those beautiful jewelries. You can also request for a short course to make your own jewelry.

45. SURFWEAR, BEACHWEAR, ACCESSORIES, AND EQUIPMENT.

You can go to Kuta or Legian to find the best surfwear and surfing accessories. The shops particularly sell international brands like Oakley, Billabong, Rip Curl, Quicksilver, and Volcom. There are also diving and snorkeling equipments. Beachwear from top brands is also available in the shops.

46. TRADITIONAL MARKET: KUTA ART SHOP, SARASWATI TRADITIONAL MARKET, AND MANY MORE

These places are where your bargaining ability is tested. Please keep in mind that when shopping in traditional markets in Bali (or elsewhere in Indonesia) you should bargain (for 10-40% lower cost). In the traditional shops or markets, you will find many local handicrafts, paintings, Bali printed T-shirts, sarong (a long piece of cloth worn wrapped around the body/or lower body and tucked under the armpits or at the waist), and other fashion items. It is the place where you can buy Balinese souvenirs with low price.

47. KRISNA BALI AND KAMPUNG NUSANTARA

The goods sold in these places are basically the same with those sold in the traditional market. However, the place is more modern with supermarket system and fix price tags. If you can't bargain, choose these places instead.

48. BATIK BALI

Batik is Indonesian traditional cloth pattern. Every area in Indonesia has their own type of batik, and so does Bali. A high quality Batik Bali is usually painted by hand (which is a way more expensive than the printed batik) whereas printed batik is usually made in a mass production with relatively lower prices.

49. BALINESE TRADITIONAL SNACKS

During your stay in Bali, it is also recommended to buy some Balinese traditional snacks. You can buy the snack in the traditional market or food stalls along the street. The most famous one is roasted salty peanuts. You can also try various of sweet traditional cake (dodol/traditional sticky rice cake) with many flavors for your choice. Traditional crackers are also familiar among tourists.

50. ART GALLERIES AND TATTOO ART SHOP

Do you want to bring a piece of art home? Bali is also the home of so many painters and tattoo artists. Many famous Hollywood artists came to purchase Balinese paintings or create some tattoos in many reputable tattoo art shops. For the price, you can choose from the lowest ($10 for a painting in Kuta Art Shop) to the most expensive one (just ask the painter for the price of their one and only masterpiece). There is also Blanco Renaissance Museum where the works of the world's famous painter, Don Antonio Blanco, are displayed (please note that many important people in the world, including Michael Jackson bought his painting).

These are just 50 things about traveling to Bali. There are still many places that cannot be described entirely in this book. But to make you happy, I will add some more tips that you must do in Bali. Spare sometimes before you head back to your home country to enjoy the famous Bali Spa. You can find so many spa places in Bali, from high-end resorts to small motels that provide you with the nice touch of Balinese organic cosmetic products. It is also highly recommended to purchase the spa products and use it at home.

While sunbathing, you can also ask some locals to do hair braiding services and have a completely new look by the time you return to the hotel. Sand massage services are also available along the Bali beaches. Although it is not a cozy place to have your body massaged, but at least you can lose your strain muscle after a long tiring activity.

OTHER HELPFUL RESOURCES

http://www.indonesia.travel/

http://www.indonesia.travel/en/destination/73/bali

http://www.bali.com/

http://www.balitourismboard.org/

Bonus Book

50 THINGS TO KNOW ABOUT PACKING LIGHT FOR TRAVEL

Pack the Right Way Every Time

Author: Manidipa Bhattacharyya

Edited by Melanie Howthorne

About The Author

Manidipa Bhattacharyya is a creative writer and editor, with an
education in English literature and Linguistics. After working in the IT
industry for seven long years she decided to call it quits and follow her
heart instead. Manidipa has been ghost writing, editing, proof reading
and doing secondary research services for many story tellers and article
writers for about three years. She stays in Kolkata, India with her
husband and a busy two year old. In her own time Manidipa enjoys
travelling, photography and writing flash fiction.

Manidipa believes in travelling light and never carries anything that she
couldn't haul herself on a trip. However, travelling with her child
changed the scenario. She seemed to carry the entire world with her for
the baby on the first two trips. But good sense prevailed and she is
again working her way to becoming a light traveler, this time with a
kid.

Introduction

*He who would travel happily
must travel light.*

-Antoine de Saint-Exupéry

Travel takes you to different places from seas and mountains to deserts and much more. In your travels you get to interact with different people and their cultures. You will, however, enjoy the sights and interact positively with these new people even more, if you are travelling light.

When you travel light your mind can be free from worry about your belongings. You do not have to spend precious vacation time waiting for your luggage to arrive after a long flight. There is be no chance of your bags going missing and the best part is that you need not pay a fee for checked baggage.

People who have mastered this art of packing light will root for you to take only one carry-on, wherever you go. However, many people can find it really hard to pack light. More so if you are travelling with children. Differentiating between "must have" and "just in case" items is the starting point. There will be ample shopping avenues at your destination which are just waiting to be explored.

This book will show you 'packing' in a new 'light' –
pun intended – and help you to embrace light
packing practices for all of your future travels.

Off to packing!

Dedication

I dedicate this book to all the travel buffs that I know,
who have given me great insights into the contents of
their backpacks.

The Right Travel Gear

1. Choose Your Travel Gear Carefully

While selecting your travel gear, pick items that are
light weight, durable and most importantly, easy to
carry. There are cases with wheels so you can drag
them along – these are usually on the heavy side
because of the trolley. Alternatively a backpack that
you can carry comfortably on your back, or even a
duffel bag that you can carry easily by hand or sling
across your body are also great options. Whatever
you choose, one thing to keep in mind is that the
luggage itself should not weigh a ton, this will give
you the flexibility to bring along one extra pair of
shoes if you so desire.

2. Carry The Minimum Number Of Bags

Selecting light weight luggage is not everything. You need to restrict the number of bags you carry as well. One carry-on size bag is ideal for light travel. Most carriers allow one cabin baggage plus one purse, handbag or camera bag as long as it slides under the seat in front. So technically, you can carry two items of luggage without checking them in.

3. Pack One Extra Bag

Always pack one extra empty bag along with your essential items. This could be a very light weight duffel bag or even a sturdy tote bag which takes up minimal space. In the event that you end up buying a lot of souvenirs, you already have a handy bag to stuff all that into and do not have to spend time hunting for an appropriate bag.

I'm very strict with my packing and have everything in its right place. I never change a rule. I hardly use anything in the hotel room. I wheel my own wardrobe in and that's it.

Charlie Watts

Clothes & Accessories

4. Plan Ahead

Figure out in advance what you plan to do on your trip. That will help you to pick that one dress you need for the occasion. If you are going to attend a wedding then you have to carry formal wear. If not, you can ditch the gown for something lighter that will be comfortable during long walks or on the beach.

5. Wear That Jacket

Remember that wearing items will not add extra luggage for your air travel. So wear that bulky jacket that you plan to carry for your trip. This saves space and can also help keep you warm during the chilly flight.

6. Mix and Match

Carry clothes that can be interchangeably used to reinvent your look. Find one top that goes well with a couple of pairs of pants or skirts. Use tops, shirts and jackets wisely along with other accessories like a scarf or a stole to create a new look.

7. Choose Your Fabric Wisely

Stuffing clothes in cramped bags definitely takes its toll which results in wrinkles. It is best to carry wrinkle free, synthetic clothes or merino tops. This will eliminate the need for that small iron you usually bring along.

8. Ditch Clothes Pack Underwear

Pack more underwear and socks. These are the things that will give you a fresh feel even if you do not get a chance to wear fresh clothes. Moreover these are easy to wash and can be dried inside the hotel room itself.

9. Choose Dark Over Light

While picking your clothes choose dark coloured ones. They are easy to colour coordinate and can last longer before needing a wash. Accidental food spills and dirt from the road are less visible on darker clothes.

10. Wear Your Jeans

Take only one pair of Jeans with you, which you should wear on the flight. Remember to pick a pair that can be worn for sightseeing trips and is equally eloquent for dinner. You can add variety by adding light weight cargoes and chinos.

11. Carry Smart Accessories

The right accessory can give you a fresh look even with the same old dress. An intelligent neck-piece, a couple of bright scarves, stoles or a sarong can be used in a number of ways to add variety to your clothing. These light weight beauties can double up as a nursing cover, a light blanket, beach wear, a modesty cover for visiting places of worship, and also makes for an enthralling game of peek-a-boo.

12. Learn To Fold Your Garments

Seasoned travellers all swear by rolling their clothes for compact and wrinkle free packing. Bundle packing, where you roll the clothes around a central object as if tying it up, is also a popular method of compact and wrinkle free packing. Stacking folded clothes one on top of another is a big no-no as it makes creases extreme and they are difficult to get rid of without ironing.

13. Wash Your Dirty Laundry

One of the ways to avoid carrying loads of clothes is to wash the clothes you carry. At some places you might get to use the laundry services or a Laundromat but if you are in a pinch, best solution is to wash them yourself. If that is the plan then carrying quick drying clothes is highly recommended, which most often also happen to be the wrinkle free variety.

14. Leave Those Towels Behind

Regular towels take up a lot of space, are heavy and take ages to dry out. If you are staying at hotels they will provide you with towels anyway. If you are travelling to a remote place, where the availability of towels look doubtful, carry a light weight travel towel of viscose material to do the job.

15. Use A Compression Bag

Compression bags are getting lots of recommendation now days from regular travellers. These are useful for saving space in your luggage when you have to pack bulky dresses. While packing for the return trip, get help from the hotel staff to arrange a vacuum cleaner.

Footwear

16. Put On Your Hiking Boots

If you have plans to go hiking or trekking during your trip, you will need those bulky hiking boots. The best way to carry them is to wear them on flight to save space and luggage weight. You can remove the boots once inside and be comfortable in your socks.

17. Picking The Right Shoes

Shoes are often the bulkiest items, along with being the dainty if you are a female. They need care and take up a lot of space in your luggage. It is advisable therefore to pick shoes very carefully. If you plan to do a lot of walking and site seeing, then wearing a pair of comfortable walking shoes are a must. For more formal occasions you can carry durable, light weight flats which will not take up much space.

18. Stuff Shoes

If you happen to pack a pair of shoes, ensure you utilize their hollow insides. Tuck small items like rolled up socks or belts to save space. They will also be easy to find.

Toiletries

19. Stashing Toiletries

Carry only absolute necessities. Airline rules dictate that for one carry-on bag, liquids and gels must be in 3.4 ounce (100ml) bottles or less, and must be packed in a one quart zip-lock bag. If you are planning to stay in a hotel, the basic things will be provided for you. It's best is to buy the rest from the local market at your destination.

20. Take Along Tampons

Tampons are a hard to find item in a lot of countries. Figure out how many you need and pack accordingly. For longer stays you can buy them online and have them delivered to where you are staying.

21. Get Pampered Before You Travel

Some avid travellers suggest getting a pedicure and manicure just the day before travelling. This not only gives you a well kept look, you also save the trouble of packing nail polish. Remember, every little bit of weight reduced adds up.

Electronics
22. Lugging Along Electronics

Electronics have a large role to play in our lives today. Most of us cannot imagine our lives away from our phones, laptops or tablets. However while travelling, one must consider the amount of weight these electronics add to our luggage. Thankfully smart phones come along with all the essentials tools like a camera, email access, picture editing tools and more. They are smart to the point of eliminating the need to carry multiple gadgets. Choose a smart phone that suits all your requirements and travel with the world in your palms or pocket.

23. Reduce the Number of Chargers

If you do travel with multiple electronic devices, you will have to bear the additional burden of carrying all their chargers too. Check if a single charger can be used for multiple devices. You might also consider investing in a pocket charger. These small devices support multiple devices while keeping you charged on the go.

24. Travel Friendly Apps

Along with smart phones come numerous apps, which are immensely helpful in our travels. You name it and you have an app for it at hand – take pictures, sharing with friends and family, torch to light dark roads, maps, checking flight/train times, find hotels and many other things. Use these smart alternatives to traditional items like books to eliminate weight and save space.

I get ideas about what's essential when packing my suitcase.

-Diane von Furstenberg

Travelling With Kids

25. Bring Along the Stroller

Kids might enjoy walking for a while but they soon tire out and a stroller is the just the right thing for them to rest in while you continue your tour. Strollers also double duty as a luggage carrier and shopping bag holder. Remember to pick a light weight, easy to handle brand of stroller. Better yet, find out in advance if you can rent a stroller at your destination.

26. Bring Only Enough Diapers for Your Trip

Diapers take up a lot of space and add to the weight of your luggage. Therefore it is advisable to carry just enough diapers to last through the trip and a few for afterwards, till you buy fresh stock at your destination. Unless of course you are travelling to a really remote area, in which case you have no choice but to carry the load. Otherwise diapers are something you will find pretty easily.

27. Take Only A Couple Of Toys

Children are easily attracted by new things in their environment. While travelling they will find numerous 'new' objects to scrutinize and play with. Packing just one favorite toy is enough, or if there is no favorite toy leave out all of them in favor of stories or imaginary games.

28. Carry Kid Friendly Snacks

Create a small snack counter in your bag to store away quick bites for those sudden hunger pangs. Depending on the child's age this could include chocolates, raisins, dry fruits, granola bars or biscuits. Also keep a bottle of water handy for your little one.

These things do not add much weight and can be adjusted in a handbag or knapsack.

29. Games to Carry

Create some travel specific, imaginary games if you have slightly grown up children, like spot the attractions. Keep a coloring book and colors handy for in-flight or hotel time. Apps on your smart phone can keep the children engaged with cartoons and story books. Older children are often entertained by games available on phones or tablets. This cuts the weight of luggage down while keeping the kids entertained.

30. Let the Kids Carry Their Load

A good thing is to start early sharing of responsibilities. Let your child pick a bag of his or her choice and pack it themselves. Keep tabs on what they are stuffing in their bags by asking if they will be using that item on the trip. It could start out being just an entertainment bag initially but with growing years they will learn to sort the useful from the superfluous. Children as little as four can maneuver a small trolley suitcase like a pro- their experience in pull along toys credit. If you are worried that you may be pulling it for them, you may want to start with a backpack.

31. Decide on Location for Children to Sleep

While on a trip you might not always get a crib at your destination, and carrying one will make life all the more difficult. Instead call ahead to see if there are any cribs or roll out beds for children. You may even put blankets on the floor. Weave them a story about camping and they will gladly sleep without any trouble.

32. Get Baby Products Delivered At Your Destination

If you are absolutely paranoid about not getting your favourite variety of diaper or brand of baby food, check out online stores like amazon.com for services in your destination city. You can buy things online ahead of your travel and get them delivered to your hotel upon arrival.

33. Feeding Needs Of Your Infants

If you are travelling with a breastfed infant, you save the trouble of carrying bottles and bottle sanitization kits. For special food, or medications, you may need to call ahead to make sure you have a refrigerator where you are staying.

34. Feeding Needs of Your Toddler

With the progression from infancy to toddler, their dietary requirements too evolve. You will have to pack some snacks for travelling time. Fresh fruits and vegetables can be purchased at your destination. Most of the cities you travel to in whichever part of the world, will have baby food products and formulas, available at the local drug-store or the supermarket.

35. Picking Clothes for Your Baby

Contrary to popular belief, babies can do without many changes of clothes. At the most pack 2 outfits per day. Pack mix and match type clothes for your little one as well. Pick things which are comfortable to wear and quick to dry.

36. Selecting Shoes for Your Baby

Like outfits, kids can make do with two pairs of comfortable shoes. If you can get some water resistant shoes it will be best. To expedite drying wet shoes, you can stuff newspaper in them then wrap

them with newspaper and leave them to dry
overnight.

37. Keep One Change of Clothes Handy

Travelling with kids can be tricky. Keep a change of
clothes for the kids and mum handy in your purse or
tote bag. This takes a bit of space in your hand
luggage but comes extremely handy in case there are
any accidents or spills.

38. Leave Behind Baby Accessories

Baby accessories like their bed, bath tub, car seat, crib
etc. should be left at home. Many hotels provide a
crib on request, while car seats can be borrowed from
friends or rented. Babies can be given a bath in the
hotel sink or even in the adult bath tub with a little bit
of water. If you bring a few bath toys, they can be
used in the bath, pool, and out of water. They can also
be sanitized easily in the sink.

39. Carry a Small Load Of Plastic Bags

With children around there are chances of a number
of soiled clothes and diapers. These plastic bags help
to sort the dirt from the clean inside your big bag.

These are very light weight and come in handy to other carry stuff as well at times.

Pack with a Purpose

40. Packing for Business Trips

One neutral-colored suit should suffice. It can be paired with different shirts, ties and accessories for different occasions. One pair of black suit pants could be worn with a matching jacket for the office or with a snazzy top for dinner.

41. Packing for A Cruise

Most cruises have formal dinners, and that formal dress usually takes up a lot of space. However you might find a tuxedo to rent. For women, a short black dress with multiple accessory options will do the trick.

42. Packing for A Long Trip Over Different Climates

The secret packing mantra for travel over multiple climates is layering. Layering traps air around your body creating insulation against the cold. The same light t-shirt that is comfortable in a warmer climate can be the innermost layer in a colder climate.

Reduce Some More Weight

43. Leave Precious Things At Home

Things that you would hate to lose or get damaged leave them at home. Precious jewelry, expensive gadgets or dresses, could be anything. You will not require these on your trip. Leave them at home and spare the load on your mind.

44. Send Souvenirs by Mail

If you have spent all your money on purchasing souvenirs, carrying them back in the same bag that you brought along would be difficult. Either pack everything in another bag and check it in the airport or get everything shipped to your home. Use an international carrier for a secure transit, but this could be more expensive than the checking fees at the airport.

45. Avoid Carrying Books

Books equal to weight. There are many reading apps which you can download on your smart phone or tab.

Plus there are gadgets like Kindle and Nook that are thinner and lighter alternatives to your regular book.

Check, Get, Set, Check Again

46. Strategize Before Packing

Create a travel list and prepare all that you think you need to carry along. Keep everything on your bed or floor before packing and then think through once again – do I really need that? Any item that meets this question can be avoided. Remove whatever you don't really need and pack the rest.

47. Test Your Luggage

Once you have fully packed for the trip take a test trip with your luggage. Take your bags and go to town for window shopping for an hour. If you enjoy your hour long trip it is good to go, if not, go home and reduce the load some more. Repeat this test till you hit the right weight.

48. Add a Roll Of Duct Tape

You might wonder why, when this book has been talking about reducing stuff, we're suddenly asking you to pack something totally unusual. This is because when you have limited supplies, duct tape is immensely helpful for small repairs – a broken bag, leaking zip-lock bag, broken sunglasses, you name it and duct tape can fix it, temporarily.

49. List of Essential Items

Even though the emphasis is on packing light, there are things which have to be carried for any trip. Here is our list of essentials:

- Passport/Visa or any other ID

- Any other paper work that might be required on a trip like permits, hotel reservation confirmations etc.

- Medicines – all your prescription medicines and emergency kit, especially if you are travelling with children

- Medical or vaccination records

- Money in foreign currency if travelling to a different country

- Tickets- Email or Message them to your phone

50. Make the Most of Your Trip

Wherever you are going, whatever you hope to do we encourage you to embrace it whole-heartedly. Take in the scenery, the culture and above all, enjoy your time away from home.

Packing and Planning Tips

A Week before Leaving

- Arrange for someone to take care of pets and water plants

- Stop mail and newspaper

- Notify Credit Card companies where you are going.

- Change your thermostat settings

- Car inspected, oil is changed, and tires have the correct pressure.

- Passports and id is up to date.

- Pay bills.

- Copy important items and download travel Apps.

- Start collecting small bills for tips

Right Before Leaving

- Clean out refrigerator.

- Empty garbage cans.

- Lock windows.

- Make sure you have the right ID with you.

- Bring cash for tips.

- Remember travel documents.

- Lock door behind you.

- Remember wallet.

- Unplug items in house and pack chargers.

Read other
Greater Than a Tourist
Books

Greater Than a Tourist San Miguel de Allende Guanajuato Mexico:
50 Travel Tips from a Local by Tom Peterson

Greater Than a Tourist – Lake George Area New York USA:
 50 Travel Tips from a Local by Janine Hirschklau

Greater Than a Tourist – Monterey California United States:
50 Travel Tips from a Local by Katie Begley

 Greater Than a Tourist – Chanai Crete Greece:
50 Travel Tips from a Local by Dimitra Papagrigoraki

Greater Than a Tourist – The Garden Route Western Cape Province
South Africa:
50 Travel Tips from a Local by Li-Anne McGregor van Aardt

Greater Than a Tourist – Sevilla Andalusia Spain:
50 Travel Tips from a Local by Gabi Gazon

Greater Than a Tourist – Kota Bharu Kelantan Malaysia:
50 Travel Tips from a Local by Aditi Shukla

Children's Book: Charlie the Cavalier Travels the World by Lisa
Rusczyk

> TOURIST

Visit Greater Than a Tourist for Free Travel Tips
http://GreaterThanATourist.com

Sign up for the Greater Than a Tourist Newsletter for discount days, new books, and travel information:
http://eepurl.com/cxspyf

Follow us on Facebook for tips, images, and ideas:
https://www.facebook.com/GreaterThanATourist

Follow us on Pinterest for travel tips and ideas:
http://pinterest.com/GreaterThanATourist

Follow us on Instagram for beautiful travel images:
http://Instagram.com/GreaterThanATourist

> TOURIST

Please leave your honest review of this book on Amazon and Goodreads. Please send your feedback to GreaterThanaTourist@gmail.com as we continue to improve the series. Thank you. We appreciate your positive and constructive feedback. Thank you.

METRIC CONVERSIONS

TEMPERATURE

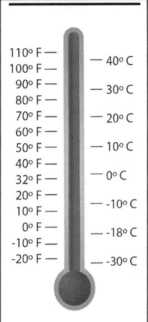

110° F — — 40° C
100° F —
90° F — — 30° C
80° F —
70° F — — 20° C
60° F —
50° F — — 10° C
40° F —
32° F — — 0° C
20° F —
10° F — — -10° C
0° F —
-10° F — — -18° C
-20° F — — -30° C

To convert F to C:
Subtract 32, and then multiply
by 5/9 or .5555.

To Convert C to F:
Multiply by 1.8
and then add 32.

32F = 0C

LIQUID VOLUME

To Convert:.................Multiply by
U.S. Gallons to Liters................ 3.8
U.S. Liters to Gallons 26
Imperial Gallons to U.S. Gallons 1.2
Imperial Gallons to Liters....... 4.55
Liters to Imperial Gallons 22
1 Liter = .26 U.S. Gallon
1 U.S. Gallon = 3.8 Liters

DISTANCE

To convert ....Multiply by
Inches to Centimeters 2.54
Centimeters to Inches 39
Feet to Meters...................... .3
Meters to Feet 3.28
Yards to Meters 91
Meters to Yards 1.09
Miles to Kilometers 1.61
Kilometers to Miles............ .62
1 Mile = 1.6 km
1 km = .62 Miles

WEIGHT

1 Ounce = .28 Grams
1 Pound = .4555 Kilograms
1 Gram = .04 Ounce
1 Kilogram = 2.2 Pounds

TRAVEL QUESTIONS

- Do you bring presents home to family or friends after a vacation?

- Do you get motion sick?

- Do you have a favorite billboard?

- Do you know what to do if there is a flat tire?

- Do you like a sun roof open?

- Do you like to eat in the car?

- Do you like to wear sun glasses in the car?

- Do you like toppings on your ice cream?

- Do you use public bathrooms?

- Did you bring your cell phone and does it have power?

- Do you have a form of identification with you?

- Have you ever been pulled over by a cop?

- Have you ever given money to a stranger on a road trip?

- Have you ever taken a road trip with animals?

- Have you ever went on a vacation alone?

- Have you ever run out of gas?

- If you could move to any place in the world, where would it be?

- If you could travel anywhere in the world, where would you travel?

- If you could travel in any vehicle, which one would it be?

- If you had three things to wish for from a magic genie, what would they be?

- If you have a driver's license, how many times did it take you to pass the test?

- What are you the most afraid of on vacation?

- What do you want to get away from the most when you are on vacation?

- What foods smells bad to you?

- What item to you bring on ever trip with you away from home?

- What makes you sleepy?

- What song would you love to hear on the radio when you're cruising on the highway?

- What travel job would you want the least?

- What will you miss most while you are away from home?

- What is something you always wanted to try?

- What is the best road side attraction that you ever saw?

- What is the farthest distance you ever biked?

- What is the farthest distance you ever walked?

- What is the weirdest thing you needed to buy while on vacation?

- What is your favorite candy?

- What is your favorite color car?

- What is your favorite family vacation?

- What is your favorite food in the world?

- What is your favorite gas station drink or food?

- What is your favorite license plate design?

- What is your favorite restaurant in the world?

- What is your favorite smell?

- What is your favorite song?

- What is your favorite sound that nature makes?

- What is your favorite thing to bring home from a vacation?

- What is your favorite vacation with friends?

- What is your favorite way to relax?

- What is your favorite weather conditions while driving?

- Where in the world would you rather never get to travel?

- Where is the farthest place you ever traveled in a car?

- Where is the farthest place you ever went North, South, East and West?

- Where is your favorite place in the world?

- Who is your favorite singer?

- Who taught you how to drive?

- Who will you miss the most while you are away?

- Who if the first person you will call when you get to your destination?

- Who brought you on your first vacation?

- Who likes to travel the most in your life?

- Would you rather be hot or cold?

- Would you rather drive above, below, or at the speed limited?

- Would you rather drive on a highway or a back road?

- Would you rather go on a train or a boat?

- Would you rather go to the beach or the woods?

TRAVEL BUCKET LIST

NOTES

Made in the USA
Las Vegas, NV
29 October 2022

58364382R00055